GLOBAL ISSUES

TERRORISM

Alex Woolf

rosen publishing's
rosen central

New York

Published in 2011 by The Rosen Publishing Group, Inc.
29 East 21st Street, New York, NY 10010

First Edition

Senior Editor: Claire Shanahan
Designer: Phipps Design
Photo Researcher: Kath Kollberg
Proofreader and Indexer: Jo Kemp

Library of Congress Cataloging-in-Publication Data

Woolf, Alex, 1964-
Terrorism / Alex Woolf. -- 1st ed.
     p. cm. -- (Global issues)
Includes bibliographical references and index.
ISBN 978-1-4488-1881-5 (library binding)
1. Terrorism--Juvenile literature. I. Title.
HV6431.W624 2011
363.325--dc22

                         2010023633

Photo Credits:
Alamy Images: p. 45. Corbis Images: p. 9; Jamal Said/ Reuters p. 20, Reuters
p. 25, p. 38, David Rubinger p. 32. Getty Images: p. 27, Taxi cover, p. 5, Hulton
Archive p. 8, p. 14, p. 18; Afp p. 11, p. 24, p. 30, p. 41, p. 42. Reuters: p. 12,
p. 21, p. 28, p. 39, p. 44. Rex Features: cover, p. 16, p. 22, p. 26, p. 34, p. 37,
p. 40, RMTS/ Keystone U.S.A. p. 35, Sipa Press p. 7, p. 10, p. 15, p. 31.

Manufactured in China
CPSIA Compliance Information: Batch #W11YA: For Further Information
Contact Rosen Publishing, New York, New York at 1-800-237-9932

Contents

Chapter 1

What Is Terrorism?

Terrorism is generally defined as the deliberate use or threat of violence against civilian targets, in pursuit of a political aim. This definition is not accepted by everyone. In fact, there is no internationally agreed definition of terrorism. The reason for this is that terrorism, in the minds of most people, is a bad thing. It is therefore understandable that groups that use "violence against civilian targets in pursuit of a political aim" do not like to describe themselves as terrorists.

One Man's Freedom Fighter...

Such groups (and their supporters) prefer to call themselves revolutionaries, freedom fighters, guerrillas, soldiers engaged in a struggle for self-determination or national liberation—anything but terrorists. Yet governments whose countries are attacked by such groups find it helpful to call them terrorists because the negative connotations of this term help to rally opinion against them—whatever the legitimacy of their cause. This problem can be summarized by the phrase, "one man's freedom fighter is another man's terrorist."

Causes and Consequences

Groups who commit politically motivated violence focus on the cause (their political goals) and ignore the consequences (the deaths of civilians). Targeted governments focus on the consequences and ignore the cause.

By focusing on the cause, terrorist groups imply that some causes are worth killing for—or that they cannot be achieved without acts of violence. But is this really the case? The Indian Independence Movement, led by Mahatma Gandhi, and the U.S. Civil Rights Movement, led by Martin Luther King, achieved their goals without resorting to violent action.

Focusing purely on the consequences of political violence is equally unsatisfactory and actually plays into the hands of terrorists, since it does not distinguish between the work of the terrorist who blows up civilians in

> ### QUOTE >
>
> "The difference between the revolutionary and the terrorist lies in the reason for which each fights. For whoever stands by a just cause and fights for the freedom and liberation of his land from the invaders, the settlers, and the colonialists, cannot possibly be called terrorist."
>
> **Yasser Arafat**, in his address to the United Nations (UN) General Assembly, 1974.

a marketplace and a wartime air raid that might achieve similar results.

Terrorists would argue that the two types of action are equivalent: they, too, regard themselves as being at war, but lack the resources to conduct a conventional military campaign and so must resort to other methods.

What Terrorism Is Not

One possible route to a satisfactory definition of terrorism is to say what terrorism is not: it is not guerilla warfare or insurgency (terrorists do not function in

The popular image of a terrorist is a masked figure armed with a gun or a bomb. Yet few people who engage in this type of activity consider themselves terrorists.

the open as armed units, engage directly with military forces, or seek to seize or hold territory); it is not crime (the purpose is political, not for personal gain); nor is it the activity of a lone operator (terrorists are organized groups). So, any definition of terrorism must describe its aims (political), its methods (violent), and how these are conducted (through small, nonmilitary, subnational organizations).

Terrorism and Warfare

There is, however, one big difference between terrorism and war: warring nations are bound by rules. The Geneva and Hague Conventions, created in the nineteenth and twentieth centuries, outlaw certain types of weapon such as chemical or biological agents, forbid the killing or imprisoning of civilians, and impose strict regulations on the treatment of military prisoners (known as prisoners or war or POWs). If these and other rules are broken, those responsible can be charged with war crimes.

Such rules have never restrained terrorists, who frequently carry out atrocities that would be labeled as war crimes if they were genuinely fighting a war. The Japanese group Aum Shinrikyo used a chemical weapon in its attack on the Tokyo subway in 1995. And in 2004, the Iraqi terrorist group al Qaeda kidnapped and beheaded civilian Nick Berg. Today, definitions of terrorism have become narrower and more specific. For example, the U.S. Department of State defines terrorism as follows: "Premeditated, politically motivated violence perpetrated [carried out] against noncombatant targets by subnational groups or clandestine [secret] agents, usually intended to influence an audience."

Justifiable Terrorism?

In the panel above, Clifford D. May points out that some people think that terrorism may be justifiable under repressive regimes if no other means of bringing about change are available—that if a group is forbidden to organize a demonstration, launch a newspaper, or form a political party, its only option may be to use violence. Others believe that violence is always wrong, whatever the circumstances. "

QUOTE >

"Based on poll results, it appears that…an increasing number of Americans have come to the conclusion that terrorism—intentional acts of violence directed at noncombatants for political purposes—is wrong, always wrong, no matter the grievance, no matter the complaint. There are, however, those who reject this principle, who are fighting…to preserve the idea that murdering other people's children may be no crime…if it's in the name of a cause they approve, or if it's against a national or ethnic group they disfavor."

Clifford D. May, *National Review Online,* 2003

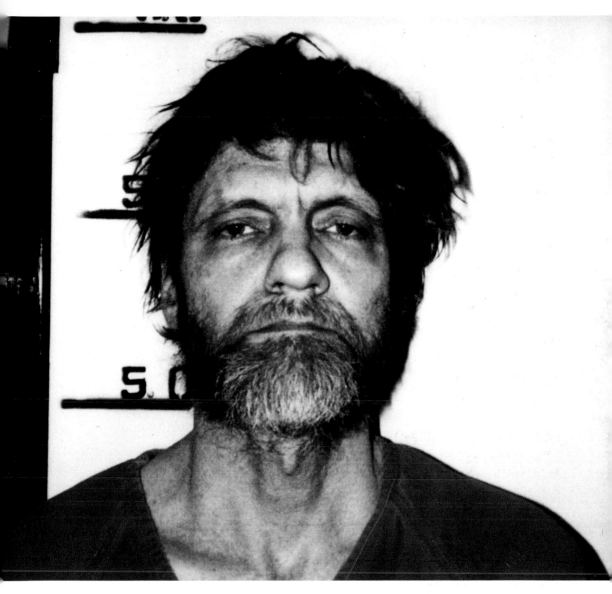

It is improbable that people will ever agree on this issue, and therefore a universally accepted definition of terrorism remains unlikely. However, for the purposes of this book, we shall use the term as it is defined at the beginning of this chapter.

Theodore Kaczynkski, the so-called Unabomber, conducted a campaign of bombings from the late 1970s to the mid-1990s. His violence was politically motivated and many would label him a terrorist.

Chapter 2

The History of Terrorism

The term "terrorism" was coined during the Reign of Terror (1793–4) during the French Revolution. At that time, it was something practiced by governments—the revolutionary government of France to be exact—as a means of imposing order and scaring opponents into submission.

The First Terrorist Groups

The term would not be applied to groups (as opposed to governments) for another century. The first of these was Narodnaya Volya, formed in 1879 to fight against tsarist rule in Russia. Yet even this group did not conform to the modern meaning of "terrorist," since it attacked the tsar only, and took great care to avoid harming civilians, including the tsar's immediate family.

Terrorism in the modern sense of the word was first carried out by an Irish nationalist group called the Irish Republican Brotherhood (IRB). Between 1883 and 1887, the IRB waged a bombing campaign against railroad stations in British cities. For the first time, civilians were being targeted. Other nationalist groups of the late nineteenth and early twentieth centuries—such as Armenians and Macedonians who fought for independence from the Ottoman Empire—tended to follow the Narodnaya Volya strategy of political assassination.

Totalitarian Terror

In the 1930s, the meaning of terrorism changed again. During this decade, the term came to be associated with the repressive measures used by totalitarian governments—notably in the Soviet Union, Germany, and Italy—against their own citizens. Opponents of these regimes were beaten up by street gangs, imprisoned and tortured by secret police, sent to forced labor camps, and often executed.

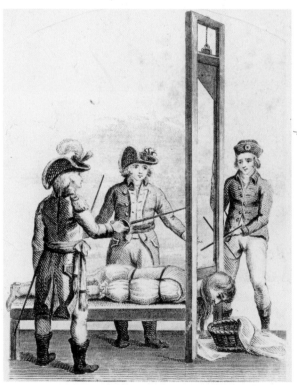

A victim undergoes execution by guillotine during the Reign of Terror in the French Revolution.

| **1793–4** The Reign of Terror in France >>> | **1879–83** Narodnaya's campaign against the Tsarist regime in Russia >>> | **1883–7** IRB campaign against British rule in Ireland >>> |

8

Anti-Colonial Campaigns

After 1945, terrorism once again became a tool of nationalist groups. This time the groups, based in Africa, Asia, and the Middle East, were struggling to free themselves from European colonial rule. Countries such as Israel and Kenya (ruled by the UK) and Algeria and Vietnam (ruled by France) won their independence at least partly because of these terrorist campaigns.

1968

In 1968, there was a big upsurge in terrorist violence. Nationalist groups such as the Palestine Liberation Organization (PLO) became more ambitious in their attacks and more global in their reach. In that year, the first aircraft hijackings were carried out.

Soldiers seize the Serb nationalist, Gavrilo Princip, after he assassinated Archduke Franz Ferdinand of Austria, sparking World War I.

Terrorism was seen as a very positive thing by the leaders of the French Revolution:

QUOTE >

"Terror is nothing but justice, prompt, severe, and inflexible; it is therefore an emanation of virtue."

Maximilien Robespierre, quoted by R. R. Palmer, *The Age of the Democratic Revolution*, 1976.

 1893–1914 Terrorist groups fight for national liberation against the Ottoman and Austrian Empires >>>

1930s State terrorism inflicted in the Soviet Union, Germany, and Italy >>>

1945–1960s Nationalist terrorist groups fight for liberation from colonial rule >>>

From 1968, terrorism became the tool not just of nationalists but of left-wing groups who sought broader political changes, such as socialist revolution and the overthrow of the entire capitalist system.

This desire for political change arose partly out of anger, especially among students, at the Vietnam War (1964–1975). These left-wing terrorists, including the Red Brigades in Italy, the Red Army Faction in West Germany, and the Angry Brigade in the UK, conducted violent attacks during the 1970s and 1980s in the hope of bringing about political change.

State-Sponsored Terrorism

During the Cold War (1945–1990), the rival superpowers secretly armed and funded terrorist groups as a means of attacking each other without risking open confrontation. The U.S.A. supported counterrevolutionary groups in places like South Vietnam, Cuba, Nicaragua, and Chile, while the Soviet Union sponsored left-wing terrorist groups in Europe.

This approach, known as state-sponsored terrorism, was also used by Iran, Iraq, Syria, and Libya in the 1980s, who funded terrorist attacks against U.S. embassies and military bases in the Middle East.

Four members of the Italian Red Brigades terrorist group are chained together and escorted by national police at the end of their second day on trial on charges of terrorism and kidnappings in 1978.

1968 Terrorism becomes more international in scope >>>

1968–1980s Heyday of left-wing terrorism >>>

1979 Islamic Revolution in Iran inspires Islamist terrorism >>>

"We must strive to export our Revolution throughout the world… for not only does Islam refuse to recognize any difference between Muslim countries, it is the champion of all oppressed people….We must make plain our stance toward the powers and superpowers….Our attitude to the world is dictated by our beliefs."

Ayatollah Khomeini, March 1980.

Ayatollah Ruhollah Musawi Khomeini became a spiritual leader to Shia Muslims and inspired millions of Islamist militants around the world. His regime ruthlessly imposed Islamic law on all aspects of life in Iran.

Islamist Terrorism

The spark for this wave of attacks against U.S. interests was the 1979 Iranian Islamic Revolution and the call to export the revolution by its leader, Ayatollah Khomeini (see panel above). Islamism, as this movement came to be known, has been the most significant force in terrorism since 1980. It aims to impose Islamic law throughout the Muslim world, leading Islamists to attack secular governments and Western interests in many Muslim countries. Islamist terrorists also frequently attack Israel and the U.S.A.

The Islamist threat reached a climax with the attacks on targets in the U.S.A. on September 11, 2001 (subsequently known as "9/11"), which left more than 3,000 dead. Such a devastating attack was unprecedented in the history of terrorism and prompted the first systematic and coordinated attempt by governments to defeat terrorism, known as the "War on Terror."

1989 Al Qaeda, founded in wake of Afghan war, supports Islamist terrorist movements throughout the Muslim world >>>

September 11, 2001 Worst-ever terrorist attack kills over 3,000, sparking War on Terror >>>

Case Study: Abu Daoud, the Man Behind the Munich Massacre

In the early hours of September 5, 1972, during the Olympic Games in Munich, West Germany, members of the Israeli Olympic team were taken hostage by the Palestinian terrorist group, Black September. Within 24 hours, the group had murdered 11 of the Israeli athletes.

Masterminding the Attack

The leader of Black September and chief planner of the Munich operation was Abu Daoud. Born in Palestine in 1937, Daoud joined the Palestinian nationalist group Fatah (part of the PLO) in 1965, and in 1970, he formed Black September, an offshoot of Fatah. In mid-1972, Daoud went to Munich to plan the attack on the Israeli Olympic team. He obtained guns and scouted the Olympic Village.

After taking the hostages, the terrorists demanded the release of Palestinian prisoners held in Israel. After several hours of tense negotiations in the full glare of the world's media, the West German authorities agreed to allow the terrorists and their hostages transportation to a nearby airport so they could leave the country. But at the airport, German police ambushed the terrorists. Five of the eight terrorists were killed, but not before they had managed to kill all the Israeli hostages.

Abu Daoud does not regret the 1972 massacre. He said, "Some of them [the Israeli athletes] had taken part in wars and killed many Palestinians."

Daoud Escapes

Israel avenged the massacre with Operation Wrath of God. Virtually all the Black September leaders were killed. Abu Daoud was shot six times in a 1981 assassination attempt in Warsaw, but survived. He admitted his involvement in the massacre in a 1999 memoir. Today, he lives in Syria.

1965 Abu Daoud joins Fatah >>> | **1970** Black September is formed >>> | **July 1972** Daoud visits Munich and plans the attack >>> | **September 5–6, 1972** Black September terrorists take Israeli Olympic team hostage and later massacre them >>>

WHAT THE WORLD THINKS...

These are three articles from newspapers around the world commenting on the Munich massacre in 1972. Compare and contrast the various viewpoints and see if you can find any more newspaper reports or other media discussing Abu Daoud.

Al-Ahram,
September 6, 1972

"[The attack was] a desperate act of people in a desperate condition."

Al-Ahram is an Egyptian newspaper.

New York Times,
September 6, 1972

"By choosing the Olympic Games as the occasion for their bloody foray, the Arab terrorists made it plain that their real target was civilized conduct among nations, not merely Israel or the Israeli athletes captured and killed yesterday."

Ma'ariv,
September 6, 1972

"We shall hit [the terrorists] at home. We shall settle our account with them and their dispatchers, with those who sheltered them in Munich, assisted in infiltrating the Olympic Village, and bringing their weapons there."

Ma'ariv is an Israeli newspaper.

1972–1981 Israel launches Operation Wrath of God, assassinating virtually all of those involved in the Munich massacre >>>

1999 Abu Daoud admits his involvement in a memoir >>>

Chapter 3

The Causes of Terrorism

Terrorism can have many different causes. Generally speaking, it can occur when a small, like-minded group of people want to bring about radical change in the way they are governed—be it a political or religious revolution or liberation from an occupying power. The three main causes of terrorism since 1945 have been nationalism, ideology, and religion.

Nationalism

Many people in the world today live, or feel that they live, under occupation. At some point in their history, their country was conquered—it may have happened recently or many centuries ago. They feel like second-class citizens in their own land, and their ethnic identity feels threatened. This can lead to movements for national self-determination—the desire of a people to govern themselves. Some of these movements are peaceful; many employ terrorist tactics.

The first major nationalist terrorist campaign was by Irgun, which fought for an independent Jewish state in British-occupied Palestine in the 1930s. Irgun's bombing campaign undermined the UK's

In 1946, the Jewish terrorist group Irgun bombed the King David Hotel in Jerusalem, which was being used as a British military headquarters, killing 91.

> QUOTE >
>
> "Our strategy consisted in turning the whole island into a single field of battle in which there was no distinction between front and rear, so that the enemy should at no time and in no place feel himself secure. The enemy never knew where and when we might strike."
>
> **George Grivas,** founder and commander of EOKA.

power and prestige, and goaded the UK into more repressive measures, alienating the general population. Irgun achieved its goal in 1947 when the British withdrew from Palestine. The 1948 War that followed led to the establishment of the state of Israel. In June 1948, David Ben-Gurion's government ended the militant movement by sinking the Irgun ship, the *Altalena*.

Irgun's strategy provided a model for nationalist terrorist struggles elsewhere, including the EOKA in British-occupied Cyprus and the FLN in French-occupied Algeria in the 1950s. Both were successful. These in turn inspired campaigns by the ANC in South Africa, the IRA in Northern Ireland, the ETA in Spain, and the PLO in Israel.

However justified they feel about their violent tactics, nationalist terrorists cannot afford to alienate their own communities, which they depend on for funding and recruitment. For this reason, they tend to avoid killing large numbers of civilians. The ETA and the IRA both sent coded warnings before their attacks to give time for evacuation.

Schoolchildren walk past a wall daubed with a pro-IRA, nationalist slogan in Northern Ireland. For 30 years, until 1998, the province was ravaged by sectarian violence.

Case Study: Abdullah Ocalan, Founder of the Kurdistan Workers Party

On February 15, 1999, the Kurdish rebel leader Abdullah Ocalan was captured by Turkish secret agents in Kenya, then flown back to Turkey for trial.

Hero or Terrorist?

Abdullah Ocalan is a hero to many Kurds, and a terrorist in the eyes of Turkey. Born in southeastern Turkey in 1948, he founded the Kurdistan Workers Party (PKK) in 1978. The aim of the movement is to found an independent Kurdish state,

Kurdistan, covering parts of Turkey, Iraq, Syria, and Iran. In 1984, the PKK embarked on a campaign of armed conflict against Turkish military, government, and civilian targets that caused the deaths of some 30,000 people over the next 15 years.

Ocalan lived in Syria until 1998, when pressure from Turkey forced the Syrian government to make him leave. Ocalan moved to Russia, then Italy and Greece, before being captured in Kenya. His arrest sparked protests from Kurds around the world. Since his capture, Ocalan has been held in solitary confinement as the only inmate of an island prison, guarded by 1,000 Turkish troops. He now argues for a peaceful solution to the Kurdish conflict with Turkey.

The recently captured Abdullah Ocalan is flown from Nairobi, Kenya, to face trial in Turkey.

1948 Abdullah Ocalan is born	**1978** Ocalan founds the PKK	**1984–1999** PKK terrorist campaign against Turkey	**1999** Ocalan is captured
>>>	>>>	>>>	>>>

WHAT THE WORLD THINKS...

These are three articles from newspapers around the world commenting on Abdullah Ocalan's capture and trial. Compare and contrast the various viewpoints and see if you can find any more newspaper reports or other media discussing Ocalan.

Turkish Daily News, February 18, 1999

"Ocalan should be punished for ordering a bloody terrorist campaign that has cost tens of thousands of lives. He has ordered attacks on villages, which resulted in the deaths of babies, pregnant women, and elderly men....Ocalan was always on TV boasting how he had ordered the murders....Now he will have to repeat all that to the court."

New York Times, February 17, 1999

"Mr. Ocalan's capture and trial should be used to help diminish this terrible conflict, not inflame it. Turkey's treatment of its Kurdish minority has undercut its democracy and damaged its international standing. Kurdish violence and terror...have provided excuses for Turkey's actions. Kurdish terrorism has obscured the legitimate grievances suffered by millions of nonviolent Kurds..."

Al Akhbar, February 23, 1999

"This stupid Turkish act has succeeded in making the Kurdish problem an international issue....If they [execute] Ocalan, human rights groups will tear them to pieces. If they do not...they will lose prestige before their people."

Al Akhbar is an Egyptian newspaper.

 2000s Ocalan calls for a ceasefire and peace negotiations, but PKK attacks continue >>>

2002 Ocalan's death sentence commuted to life imprisonment >>>

Ideology

People who feel very angry about the political system they live under may occasionally be stirred to form terrorist groups. There are two major forms of ideological terrorism: left-wing and right-

Christian Klar, a former terrorist with the Red Army Faction, a violent left-wing terrorist group in Germany that operated from 1970 to 1998.

wing. Left-wing terrorists desire radical political or social change, while right-wing terrorists wish to preserve traditional ways

1968–1980s Heyday of left-wing terrorism >>>	**1973** Abortion is made legal in the U.S.A., sparking a surge in right-wing terrorism >>>	**1991** Collapse of Soviet Union leads to demise of many left-wing groups >>>

of life, which they see as under threat. Left-wing terrorism emerged as a force in 1968, influenced by the New Left movement, which called for mass protest against the established order. The U.S. military involvement in Vietnam caused great anger, especially among the young, and sparked large-scale student demonstrations in many U.S. and European cities.

For some, student activism was not enough—real political change was only possible through a sustained campaign of violence. They formed groups like the Weathermen (U.S.A.), the Red Army Faction (West Germany), and Direct Action (Canada). By the early 1990s, many had ceased operations. Counterterrorist action, diminishing support, and the collapse of the Soviet Union (a secret supporter of many of these groups) led to their demise.

Left-wing terrorist violence is usually selective and restrained, involving kidnapping and assassinating leaders or the bombing of government or commercial buildings. They see themselves as part of a revolutionary vanguard, which they hope will inspire a mass revolution. Most are opposed to deliberately taking innocent life.

Right-wing terrorists hate the idea of change as much as left-wing terrorists loathe the status quo. They are often fiercely patriotic, racist, and homophobic. They fear the progressive policies of liberal governments, which encourage immigration and promote the rights of women, ethnic minorities, and

homosexuals. In the U.S.A., right-wing groups are often associated with fundamentalist Christian beliefs. In Europe, extreme nationalism is a much stronger factor than religion. In August 2006, a right-wing terrorist cell in Russia detonated a bomb in a Moscow market frequented by foreign traders and customers, killing 13 people.

Right-wing terrorist violence tends to be on a small scale, with little evidence of planning or organization. It takes the form of attacks on members of ethnic minorities, their places of worship, and their cemeteries. Homosexuals—and, in the U.S.A., abortion clinics—have also been targeted.

QUOTE >

"As crazy as it might seem, the plan in a few words was this: first phase, armed propaganda….Second phase, that of armed support…. Third phase, the civil war and victory. In essence, we were the embryo, the skeleton of the future …the ruling class of tomorrow in a communist society."

Patrizio Peci of the Red Brigades, an Italian left-wing terrorist group.

Religious Terrorism and Islamism

There have been religious terrorists since ancient times. The Zealots were a Jewish group fighting the Roman occupation of Palestine, and the Assassins were an extreme Muslim sect of the eleventh to thirteenth centuries. In the 1970s, extremist rabbi Meir Kahane inspired a number of Jewish terrorist groups, such as the Jewish Defense League. In the 1990s, Christian terrorist groups such as Army of God launched bombing campaigns against abortion clinics in the southern U.S.A.

However, by far the most potent force in religious terrorism today is Islamism, an extreme interpretation of Islam that calls for the establishment of sharia law in Muslim countries and a worldwide jihad (struggle) against the hostile and decadent West.

The main inspiration for Islamism was the 1979 Iranian Revolution, which created the world's first Islamist state. Another inspiration was the victory by

Students at a university in Beirut, Lebanon, run by the Shi-ite Islamist group, Hezbollah, listen to a speech by the organization's leader, Sayyed Hassan Nasrallah.

QUOTE >

"These events have divided the world into two sides: the side of believers and the side of infidels, may God keep you away from them.... Every Muslim has to rush to make his religion victorious. The winds of faith have come."

Osama bin Laden, October 2001.

Osama bin Laden is today the world's most notorious terrorist. His ultimate goal is to re-establish the caliphate (a united Islamic empire).

Islamic forces in the Afghan war against the Soviet Union (1978–1989), which spawned the international terrorist network, al Qaeda. By 2004, Islamist groups comprised nearly half the total number of active terrorist groups in the world.

Since 1991, Islamist groups have been responsible for the vast majority of serious, high-casualty terrorist attacks around the world. This is because, unlike nationalist or ideological terrorists, Islamists are less concerned about courting public sympathy. They see themselves as answerable only to God. Because Islamists are driven by their faith, religious justification for their activities is essential and they seek blessings known as *fatwas*

from Muslim clerics for all their attacks. All those who are not followers of their extreme faith are viewed as infidels, and potential targets. Islamists are not interested in negotiation or compromise, as other types of terrorist have been. As Antar Zouabri, leader of the Algerian Islamist group GIA, said, "God does not negotiate or engage in discussion."

The most effective Islamist leaders, such as al Qaeda's Osama bin Laden, have sought to portray their struggle as a "clash of civilizations," tempting all Muslims to make a choice between their faith and subservience to the West. Bin Laden even went so far as to declare war against the West in 1996 and 1998, urging Muslims to kill Americans and their allies.

2001 Over 3,000 killed in New York in an attack by al Qaeda >>> 2002 Over 180 killed in Bali, Indonesia, by Islamists with links to al Qaeda >>> 2003 191 killed in Madrid, Spain, by Islamists with links to al Qaeda >>>

21

Case Study: Mohamed Atta, Suicide Pilot in 9/11 Attacks

On September 11, 2001, 19 suicide terrorists hijacked four passenger airliners in the U.S.A. Two of the planes were flown into the World Trade Center in New York City, another into the Pentagon near Washington, DC, and the fourth crashed into a field in Pennsylvania. More than 3,000 people died in the 9/11 attacks.

An Intelligent Man

Egyptian-born graduate Mohamed Atta moved to Germany in 1992 to study urban planning. While he was there, Atta became increasingly religious and was recruited into al Qaeda. Friends described him as an intelligent man with religious beliefs, angry about Western policy toward the Middle East. After receiving training in Afghanistan, he moved to the U.S.A. in early 2000, one of a number picked for an ambitious terrorist attack.

"We Have Some Planes"

On the morning of September 11, Atta boarded American Airlines Flight 11, which departed at 7:59 a.m. At 8:24 a.m., air traffic controllers heard Atta's voice: "We have some planes. Just stay quiet and you will be okay." Atta is believed to have been flying the plane when it crashed into the North Tower of the World Trade Center 23 minutes later, killing all on board.

Mohamed Atta, who received his flight training in Florida, was believed to have been at the controls of American Airlines Flight 11, the first plane to crash into the World Trade Center on September 11, 2001.

Among Atta's belongings, U.S. authorities found a list of instructions, such as, "You should feel complete tranquility, because the time between you and your marriage in heaven is very short" and "You must make your knife sharp and you must not discomfort your animal during the slaughter."

| **1968** Mohamed Atta is born >>> | **1992** Atta moves to Germany to study >>> | **1995** Atta becomes increasingly religious following a pilgrimage to Mecca >>> | **1998** Atta forms an al Qaeda cell in Hamburg >>> |

WHAT THE WORLD THINKS...

These are three articles from newspapers around the world commenting on 9/11. Compare and contrast the various viewpoints and see if you can find any more newspaper reports or other media discussing the terrorist attack and Mohamed Atta's part in it.

Robert Kagan, Washington Post, September 11, 2001

"We are at war now. We have suffered the first, devastating strike. Certainly, it is not the last. The only question is whether we will now take this war seriously, as seriously as any war we have ever fought. Let's not be daunted by the mysterious and partially hidden identity of our attackers.... We should pour the resources necessary into a global effort to hunt them down and capture or kill them."

Al-Ahram, September 13, 2001

"In spite of its overwhelming might, the United States has proved itself incapable of preserving its own peace and security. Indeed, it has managed to turn the love and admiration that peoples around the world once felt for America...into universal suspicion and mistrust, a transformation that is the result of Washington's misuse of power and abuse of the moral foundations upon which it built its civilization."

Al-Ahram is an Egyptian newspaper.

Le Monde, September 12, 2001

"In this tragic moment, when words seem so inadequate to express the shock people feel, the first thing that comes to mind is this: we are all Americans!"

Le Monde is a French newspaper.

1999 Atta receives training in an al Qaeda camp in Afghanistan >>> | **2000** Atta moves to U.S.A. and takes flying lessons >>> | **September 11, 2001** Atta flies a passenger plane into the North Tower of the World Trade Center, New York City >>>

Chapter 4

The Impact of Terrorism

The immediate impact of terrorism is unmistakeable: it causes shock, fear, and anger among those targeted, and for the terrorists and their supporters, a sense of triumph and elation. Does terrorism work?

If, by "working," one means the fulfillment of their goals—be it national self-determination or religious or political revolution—then one has to conclude that the vast majority of terrorism fails.

Consciousness Raising

But there are other ways that terrorism achieves its goals. Palestinian terrorism, for example, has so far failed to produce a Palestinian state, yet it has raised global consciousness of its cause and won some sympathy for the Palestinian people from some parts of the world. In contrast, the Armenians, Tibetans, Kashmiris, and Kosovo Albanians, with equally worthy claims to national self-determination, have not used terrorism to the same extent, if at all, and their causes are consequently less well known.

Terrorist groups that have been most effective, in terms of both consciousness raising and achievement of goals, have been nationalist groups. Irgun, EOKA, and FLN won their struggles. The PLO, ETA, and the IRA have drawn attention to their causes and won concessions from their enemies.

Nationalist terrorist groups tend to achieve their aims because—unlike ideological terrorists—they have deep roots in their communities from which they can draw recruits and funds. Also, their image as rebels fighting an occupying power (whether that is a fair characterization or not) tends to win international sympathy. Ideological and religious terrorists, in contrast, usually have vague, visionary goals—such as the overthrowing of capitalism or the restoration of the caliphate—which are harder for most people to identify with.

Palestinian terrorist Leila Khaled had no doubts about the ultimate goal of her movement. "We shall win," she wrote in 1973, "because we are determined to achieve victory."

Carlos "the Jackal" raises his fist as he courts publicity during an appearance at the trial of his former accomplice, Hans-Joachim Kleinin, in Paris in 2000.

Headlines

Most terrorists cannot realistically expect to achieve their ultimate goals so, for many, the publicity and attention generated by an attack becomes a goal in itself, and the measure by which they judge their progress as a movement. Left-wing terrorist Carlos "the Jackal" and Islamist Ramzi Yousef, for example, kept files of newspaper clippings about themselves and their activities. The impact of terrorism, for such people, is measured in the headlines it generates.

QUOTE >

"The main thing was that you felt you were able to influence the world about you, instead of experiencing it passively. It was this ability to make an impact on the reality of everyday life that was important, and obviously still is important."

Susana Ronconi of the Red Brigades.

The Impact on Survivors

Terrorist attacks are, by their nature, deeply shocking. Beyond the immediate trauma of the attack, survivors may have to face further challenges, such as disability or bereavement. In the long run, they may suffer from guilt, fear, or depression. Victims of kidnappings or hijacks often face years of traumatic memories about their ordeal.

> **QUOTE >**
>
> "I was actually really unhappy that I'd survived—for a long time. As far as I was concerned, the easier thing would have been if I'd died. I felt… isolated. I also felt a huge responsibility for all the families of my friends who were killed, in the sense that I was the only survivor. That was awful."
>
> **Polly Miller**, a British survivor of the terrorist bombing in Bali on October 12, 2002. She suffered burns to 43 percent of her body. Her husband and best friend were both killed.

The Effect on Society

Terrorism can cause existing divisions in society to deepen, since opinions harden either in sympathy with the terrorists or against them. These divisions most often

Norman Kember, a British peace campaigner, was taken hostage by a terrorist group in Iraq on November 28, 2005. He was rescued by UK forces on March 23, 2006.

occur along ethnic or religious lines, as they did between Catholics and Protestants in Northern Ireland during the Troubles (1969–1998) and as they still do between Sunni and Shia Muslims in Iraq since 2003.

As tensions increase between communities during a terrorist campaign, they can spill over into a general distrust of people from a particular background. For instance, in the year following 9/11, there was a noticeable increase in abusive and sometimes violent attacks on Muslims across Europe.

The Economic Impact

Terrorism can also adversely affect the economies of countries where terrorist attacks take place. A sustained bombing campaign can cause a fear of public places and a consequent slump in commercial activity in city centers. Stores, cafes, and businesses can close down, and foreign investors can move out. This happened, for example, in Jerusalem, Israel, during the Palestinian uprising known as the Al-Aqsa Intifada (2000–2005).

Terrorist attacks on centers of tourism can be particularly devastating for local economies. After terrorists killed 58 tourists in Luxor, Egypt, in November 1997, tourism to Egypt slumped by 13.8 percent and tourist spending decreased by 45 percent. Tourism accounts for 19 percent of Egypt's export earnings, so this attack hit the economy very hard.

One of the main trading streets in Baghdad, Iraq, lies empty and filled with garbage a month after the fall of Saddam Hussein's regime.

Case Study: Priscilla Salyers, Survivor of the 1995 Oklahoma City Bombing

On April 19, 1995, Timothy McVeigh, an army veteran with a hatred for the U.S. government, bombed the Alfred P. Murrah Federal Building, a government office building in Oklahoma City, Oklahoma. The attack claimed 168 lives and left more than 800 injured.

Survivors comfort each other in the aftermath of the Oklahoma City bombing. The blast destroyed a third of the building and damaged numerous buildings and cars in the area.

An Ordinary April Morning

U.S. Customs employee Priscilla Salyers arrived at her office on the fifth floor of the Alfred P. Murrah Federal Building at 8:05 a.m. on the morning of April 19. At 9:02 a.m., she was at her desk working at her computer when her colleague, Paul Ice, leaned over to ask a question. She didn't hear it. At that moment, a powerful explosion ripped through the building. Then she felt herself falling. Priscilla plunged three floors. Paul died instantly, but somehow Priscilla survived. She lay face down, trapped under tons of rubble, with broken ribs and a punctured lung. Breathing was difficult, but she dug out an air pocket for herself. She tried to move something that was pressed against her chest, before realizing it was the hand of someone trapped beneath her. She lay there for four and a half hours before being rescued.

Moving Forward

Priscilla made a full recovery from her injuries, with her story even becoming a movie, *Oklahoma City: A Survivor's Story*. In June 2001, she watched the execution of the bomber, Timothy McVeigh, on closed-circuit TV. Interviewed beforehand, she said, "I feel that there are going to be some people who will feel a sense of healing once he is dead. There are people like me [for whom] it will not matter. We are already moving forward in our lives. We are not going to allow him to control us."

1988 Priscilla Salyers starts her job at U.S. Customs. Timothy McVeigh enlists in the U.S. Army >>>

1991 McVeigh is awarded the Bronze Star Medal for services in the Gulf War >>>

WHAT THE WORLD THINKS...

These are three articles from publications in North and South America commenting on the Oklahoma City bombing in 1995. Compare and contrast the various viewpoints and see if you can find any more newspaper reports or other media discussing the event.

Betty Tramel,
The Oklahoman,
April 20, 1995

"Some day, hopefully sooner than later, we will be able to take in a ball game again.... It will help the healing. But it won't make the hurt go away. Terrorism doesn't just break bones and slice skin and crush skulls. It breaks your heart and brands your soul."

Estrategia,
April 24, 1995

"The world received with horror, indignation, and pain the news of the bombing attack against a federal building in Oklahoma City..."

Estrategia is a Chilean newspaper.

Time,
May 1, 1995

"This much is certain: the courage of the bereaved and the heroism of the rescuers in Oklahoma City are the stuff of true patriotism."

 1992 McVeigh receives an honorable discharge from the U.S. Army. He becomes a drifter and drug user, attracted to right-wing, antigovernment causes >>>

April 19, 1995 McVeigh detonates a bomb outside the Murrah Federal building in Oklahoma City >>>

Chapter 5

Responses to Terrorism

Governments use a range of measures to deal with a terrorist threat. These include negotiation, covert action, international cooperation, and outright force.

Talking with Terrorists

Governments do not often like to be seen negotiating directly with terrorists. This can be distasteful to the public, particularly those who have lost relatives to terrorist attacks. Offering them a seat at the negotiating table confers a level of legitimacy to terrorists, encouraging them (and others) in the belief that violence can reap political rewards.

Nevertheless, there are times when governments are obliged to engage with terrorists, for example, during a kidnapping or hijacking. When Air France Flight 8969 was hijacked by members of GIA in December 1994, French prime minister Edouard Balladur was personally involved in negotiations for passengers' release.

Talking with terrorists in order to reach a long-term settlement is more politically sensitive, but governments may do this in secret if, say, they see no way of defeating the terrorists by other means. The UK government conducted secret negotiations with the IRA in the early 1990s, and the Sri Lankan government did the same with the terrorist group, the Tamil Tigers, in the 2000s.

Former archenemies, Ian Paisley, leader of the Democratic Unionist Party, and Gerry Adams, leader of republican party Sinn Fein, agreed in 2007 to work with each other in the Northern Ireland Assembly, following the 1998 Good Friday Agreement.

1981 The U.S. resolves Iran hostage crisis (when U.S. diplomats were held hostage in Tehran for 444 days) through negotiation >>>

1987 The French government pays $330 million for the release of French hostages in Beirut >>>

Covert Action

Many governments establish specialist counterterrorist agencies in order to disrupt terrorist networks, freeze terrorist assets, and preempt attacks. They use surveillance techniques to monitor telephone and email traffic between suspects, or plant moles (informers) in suspected terrorist cells.

Because terrorist cells are usually well hidden, governments sometimes find it necessary to give police extra powers to deal with the threat. This can include controversial measures that affect civil liberties, such as the introduction of identity cards or the detaining of suspects for lengthy periods without trial.

International Cooperation

Today, terrorism is a global phenomenon, and effective counterterrorism requires governments to coordinate with each other and pool intelligence. The United Nations (UN) plays a valuable role in this coordination. Between 1963 and 2001,

Since 2001, the U.S. government has imprisoned terrorism suspects for long periods without trial at Guantanamo Bay in Cuba.

the UN passed 12 major counterterrorism resolutions. Since 9/11, there has been a much greater willingness among governments to cooperate with each other to confront terrorism.

> QUOTE >
>
> "Terrorism is…a moral challenge to legitimate political and social life. It requires a sober, consistent, and sometimes forceful response by all nations, which should observe a policy of 'no concessions to terrorism.'"
>
> **Christopher C. Harmon Cass,** *Terrorism Today*, 2000.

1993 Oslo Accords between Israel and the PLO signed in Washington. DC >>>

2001 UN Security Council Resolution 1373 is adopted, aiming to place barriers on the movement, organization, and fund-raising activities of terrorist groups >>>

31

Case Study: Yonatan Netanyahu, Leader of the Raid on Entebbe

On the night of July 3, 1976, Israeli special forces conducted a daring rescue mission to free hostages held on Air France Flight 139 at Entebbe Airport in Uganda.

Air France Flight 139 was hijacked on June 27, 1976, by the PFLP-EO, a

said they would start killing the 103 remaining hostages if demands for Palestinian prisoner releases weren't met by Israel.

On July 2, while negotiations continued, a rescue attempt was approved by the Israeli government. A team of Israeli commandos, led by Yonatan Netanyahu, landed at Entebbe at 1 p.m. on July 3. A Mercedes with accompanying Land Rovers emerged from the transport aircraft and drove toward the airport building. The troops were posing as Idi Amin and his escort. They burst into the airport building, shouting "get down" in Hebrew and English, then shot the hijackers. Grenades were flung into an adjoining room, killing

A member of the rescue squadron is lfted up by the crowd on his return to Israel.

Palestinian terrorist group, and the RZ, a left-wing German group. The plane landed at Entebbe Airport in Uganda—Ugandan leader Idi Amin openly supported the hijackers—and non-Israeli/non-Jewish passengers were released. The hijackers

the remaining hijackers. Three hostages, 45 Ugandan troops, and all six hijackers were killed in the raid. Netanyahu was killed by a Ugandan sniper as they made their way from the airport. The raid was renamed Operation Yonatan in his honor.

> **June 27, 1976** Terrorists hijack Air France Flight 139 en route from Israel to France >>> | **June 29, 1976** The terrorists call for the release of 53 Palestinian political prisoners held in Israel and other countries, setting a deadline of July 1 >>>

WHAT THE WORLD THINKS...

These are two U.S. commentaries on the Israeli rescue operation at Entebbe in 1976. Compare and contrast the viewpoints and see if you can find any more newspaper reports or other media discussing Yonatan Netanyahu and his part in the raid.

Time,
July 12, 1976

"As Israelis awakened to the news of the rescue, excitement and pride rippled through the country. Gone was the humiliating feeling of helplessness with which they had lived through most of the week, as it increasingly appeared that the skyjackers would get their way."

Drew Middleton,
New York Times,
July 5, 1976

"Strategic and tactical surprise, achieved through deception, were seen...as the key to Israel's success in the raid on Entebbe airport.... Strategic surprise was won by giving the impression that Israel intended to negotiate for the lives of the hostages...tactical surprise was gained by creating diversions with bombs, grenades, and flares at the opposite side of the airport..."

July 1, 1976 The Israeli Defense Force (IDF) plan a rescue operation. Non-Israeli/non-Jewish passengers are released. The terrorists extend the deadline to July 4 >>>

July 4, 1976 By 12:40 a.m., the Israeli commandos and rescued hostages begin their return to Israel >>>

33

The second plane crashes into the Twin Towers in New York City on September 11, 2001. The events of that day sparked the War on Terror.

The War on Terror

The 9/11 attacks on the U.S.A. shocked the world. In their immediate aftermath, President George W. Bush declared a "War on Terror." This war would be fought on many fronts: economic and diplomatic pressure would be placed on governments that supported terrorists; terrorist assets would be frozen; and, in extreme cases, military force would be used. The international community was united in support for the U.S. position in the wake of the attacks. The United Nations passed Resolution 1373, obliging all states to criminalize assistance for terrorist activities, deny support and shelter to terrorists, and share information about terrorist groups.

The first military target of the war was the Taliban, the Islamist regime in Afghanistan, which gave support and shelter to al Qaeda, the terrorist network responsible for 9/11. The Taliban was overthrown by early 2002. However, from 2003, they began an effective insurgency that embroiled coalition troops in a lengthy conflict.

September 12, 2001 George W. Bush launches the War on Terror >>>

October 4, 2001 Operation Active Endeavor launches to prevent movement of terrorists or WMD in the Mediterranean >>>

October 7, 2001 U.S.-led coalition begins bombing of Afghanistan >>>

34

Iraq War

In March 2003, a new front in the War on Terror was opened when a mainly U.S.-British force invaded Iraq. The invasion was launched because Iraqi leader Saddam Hussein was suspected of developing weapons of mass destruction (WMD), which he may have shared with terrorists; he had flouted numerous UN resolutions; he had suspected links with al Qaeda; and he had gassed and executed large numbers of his own people.

The Iraq War marked the first serious division among coalition partners in the War on Terror, with several countries opposing the invasion. Saddam's connections with al Qaeda were never proved and many saw it as a distraction from the War on Terror. In the aftermath of the successful invasion, it was discovered that Saddam did not, in fact, have WMD. The occupation by coalition forces sparked a major insurgency, drawing in al Qaeda fighters from abroad. By mid-2007, much of the country remained ungovernable and subjected to almost daily terrorist attacks.

Coalition troops check for land mines in the province of Kandahar in southern Afghanistan, in 2006.

 October 26, 2001 U.S. Patriot Act passed, expanding powers of law enforcement agencies to fight terrorism. Civil liberties groups are concerned >>>

2004–6 Diminishing support for the War on Terror by a number of countries, including France, Germany, and Russia >>>

Chapter 6

Terrorism and the Media

One of terrorism's main goals is to attract publicity for its cause. Terrorists have become adept at maximizing media coverage, which is why they bomb city centers at busy times of the day. Sometimes, terrorists are so concerned about publicity, they will modify their actions to suit the media. During his 1975 kidnapping of Arab oil ministers in Vienna, Carlos "the Jackal" awaited the arrival of television camera crews before making his dramatic escape with the hostages.

The media, for its part, is unable to ignore terrorist attacks for their shock value and human stories—this kind of news sells newspapers and increases ratings. However, many would argue that the style of coverage is not always responsible. In the case of kidnappings, media preoccupation with the fate of hostages can play into terrorists' hands by placing undue pressure on governments to negotiate.

The Hostage Show

In one case, media coverage bore uncomfortable resemblance to a reality television show. When the Islamist group, Abu Sayyaf, took 21 hostages, including a German family, in the Philippines in April 2000, the drama played out every night on German TV. Over the next eight months, viewers became intimately acquainted with the hostages and their kidnappers and the lines between information and entertainment became blurred.

Today's 24-hour rolling TV news requires constant stories. With numerous competing news networks fighting to maintain their ratings, there is great pressure to find the scoop. Concerns about responsibility and accuracy are often set aside in the race to "go live on air." Following the 1995 Oklahoma City bombing, the media reported an Arab-looking man as a possible suspect, resulting in Arab Americans in Oklahoma becoming targets of physical attacks and insults.

> **QUOTE >**
>
> "The terrorists exploited the normal lust of the media—particularly TV—for breaking events of international impact….Media competition, always brutal, is especially fierce in this atmosphere, partly because the public is more attentive, partly because media stardom may be at stake for some."
>
> **Fred Barnes,** U.S. newspaper columnist, writing in the wake of a 1985 hostage crisis.

1972 Munich massacre during Olympic Games receives worldwide media coverage >>>

1985 Hijacking of TWA 847: the media focus on the plight of the hostages is criticized for pressuring the government into negotiating with the terrorists >>>

Legitimizing Terrorism?

In some cases, the media has been criticized for giving status and legitimacy to terrorists. In August 2005, the U.S. TV network ABC broadcast an interview with Chechen terrorist Shamil Basayev, who had been responsible for the 2004 Beslan

Initial reporting of the terrorist attacks on September 11, 2001, was widely praised, but the scenes were then replayed repeatedly on TV, upsetting many.

school siege in Russia, in which over 330 people died, prompting protests from the Russian government.

So does the media play into the terrorists' hands? Journalists would say "no." Although they do give terrorists publicity, it is rarely, if ever, favorable. However, others argue that the extensive coverage given to terrorist incidents runs the risk of overemphasizing the threat, adding to public fear and insecurity.

BREAKING NEWS
REPORTS: PART OF WORLD TRADE CENTER TOWER COLLAPSES
CNN

1993 World Trade Center bombing, the first major terrorist attack on U.S. soil, shocks the country >>>

October 2001 Media hysteria over the anthrax letter scare: scary scenarios are discussed involving the deaths of thousands, but only five people actually die in the attacks >>>

Terrorists and the Internet

Since the 1990s, the Internet has given terrorists unprecedented power to spread their propaganda, allowing them to bypass the traditional media altogether.

The Internet has huge advantages for terrorists. It is difficult to censor or shut down; messages can be sent anonymously, quickly, and cheaply; and it gives terrorists total control over how they portray themselves and their actions. The Internet is also a powerful fund-raising tool and a valuable source of information.

The first terrorist group to harness the power of the Internet were the left-wing Zapatistas in Mexico. As well as using it to pass messages to supporters around the world, they have used it since the early 1990s to wage electronic civil disobedience campaigns, including "mail bombs" and "virtual sit-ins"—flooding mailboxes and overworking web sites so they can no longer function.

> **QUOTE >**
>
> "Dear Donor: Please tell us the field in which you prefer your money to be spent on, such as: martyrdom attacks; buying weapons for the mujahadeen; training the youth; or inventing and developing missiles, mortars [and] explosives."
>
> Message that appeared on a web site affiliated to Hamas.

Members of the Zapatista National Liberation Army at a rally in Tuxtla Gutiérrez, Mexico. The Zapatistas have been using the Internet to raise support as well as to cause disturbances since the early 1990s.

SITE Intelligence Group

This image comes from the SITE Institute, a U.S.-based group that monitors terror messages. Al Qaeda aired this video on the internet showing a message from its leader Osama bin Laden on the sixth anniversary of the September 11 attacks.

The Zapatista campaign inspired Islamist groups who, in the early 2000s, used hackers to attack Israeli government web sites in what came to be called the Internet intifada or e-jihad. Although no one has yet been killed by this cyberterrorism, it does have the potential to create massive administrative and economic disruption in the future as we rely increasingly on electronic forms of communication.

The Tamil Tigers, a nationalist terrorist group in Sri Lanka, have used the Internet to mobilize support among the many Tamils living abroad. They also used it effectively to embarrass the Sri Lankan army. In 1996, the army claimed it had repelled a Tamil attack on its base at Mullaitivu with minimal casualties. TamilNet disproved this claim by posting live satellite pictures from the scene showing that the camp had been captured and that more than 1,000 Sri Lankan soldiers had been killed in the process.

2001 Hezbollah claims it is receiving 40,000 visits to its sites per month >>>

2001 A Saudi graduate student in the U.S.A. is convicted of using the Internet to raise funds for terrorist organizations >>>

Today, virtually all terrorist groups have web sites. Islamist terrorist groups use the web for offensive operations, such as sending coded instructions to operatives through steganography on innocent-looking web sites. They also use it for propaganda, fund-raising and recruitment.

At the forefront is the Lebanon-based Shi'ite group, Hezbollah, which has about 20 different sites in three languages. Another is al Qaeda, which uses the Internet for terrorist training and

instruction, operational planning for attacks, and intelligence gathering. Since the loss of their Afghan base in 2002, the web has offered al Qaeda a "virtual base" to continue communicating with their fighters, followers, and supporters.

The Internet has even been used by terrorists to lure victims to their deaths. In 2000, 16-year-old Israeli Ofir Rahum was befriended by a woman posing as an Israeli named Sali in an Internet chat room. In fact, she was Fatah operative Amneh Muna. She invited him for a romantic rendezvous in Jerusalem. The bus took them to Palestinian-controlled Ramallah, where Ofir was killed.

A still from a 2004 videotaped announcement by al Qaeda's second-in-command, Dr. Ayman al-Zawahiri. He warns that the U.S.A. will "bleed to death" if it stays in Iraq.

1991 Al-Manar, the Hezbollah TV station, begins broadcasting >>> | **1995** PKK founds Med-TV >>> | **1998** Al Qaeda releases professionally produced DVD of its attack on the U.S. destroyer, the *USS Cole* >>>

40

The news desk at Hezbollah's al-Manar TV station. Al-Manar provides daily news bulletins in Arabic, English, and French. It has offices in five Middle Eastern countries and correspondents in Russia, Europe, and North Africa.

Video Production

Al Qaeda and other groups have used DVDs and professionally produced video clips to project their message to supporters and potential recruits. These include videotaped battles, as well as gruesome videos of hostage beheadings. The video showing the 2002 execution of the U.S. journalist, Daniel Pearl, was shot with a blue background to enable the terrorists to splice in images of Israeli army actions against Palestinian civilians. This set Pearl's death in context with the wider Islamist jihad.

Private Television Stations

Hezbollah was the first terrorist group to have its own television station. Al-Manar was established in 1991 and today broadcasts its anti-Israel, anti-U.S.

propaganda via satellite 24 hours a day. It is now the fifth most popular station among Middle Eastern Arabs. Its battle footage and reports are even watched by Israeli soldiers" families to get a view uncensored by the Israeli authorities.

The widespread use of the Internet, video production, and satellite broadcasting have allowed terrorists to bypass traditional media, and today, terrorist web sites are regularly consulted and cited by the traditional media.

 2002 Video released of Daniel Pearl's execution >>> | **2004** During Beslan school siege in Russia, the hostages are constantly filmed by one of the terrorists >>>

Case Study: Kenneth Bigley, Held Hostage by Terrorists in Iraq

Kenneth Bigley was a civil engineer from Liverpool, UK, working on a reconstruction project in Baghdad. In September 2004, he and two U.S. citizens were kidnapped by an Islamist group called Tawhid and Jihad, led by the Jordanian terrorist, Abu Musab al-Zarqawi.

Media Pressure

Bigley's incarceration and attempts by his family to obtain his release received extensive coverage in the UK media. When the terrorists posted videos on Islamist web sites showing Bigley pleading for his life, these were shown on UK TV news channels. All this was enough to turn Bigley's fate into the UK's major political issue for the three weeks of his confinement.

Some claimed that the UK government became a hostage to the situation. The prime minister and foreign secretary were in personal contact with the Bigley family, reassuring them that everything possible was being done to help him.

In one of the videos, Kenneth Bigley appealed directly to the prime minister: "I need you to help me now, Mr. Blair,

because you are the only person on God's earth who can help me."

No Alternative?

Bigley was beheaded on October 7, 2004. After his death, some criticized the UK media for its coverage. Broadcaster Andrew Neil said, "We are playing into the hands of the terrorists….It seems to me they're rather sophisticated: they can see our TV on the web…and they know how it's playing. Having said all that, I see no alternative. In a free country with a free press, we have to cover the news."

A still from one of the videos released by Bigley's captors, showing him kneeling before them. Media coverage of the story placed intense pressure on the UK government.

September 16, 2004 Bigley and two others are kidnapped >>>

September 18, 2004 Video released of the three men kneeling in front of the terrorists" banner >>>

September 20/21, 2004 The two U.S. hostages are beheaded. Videos of the killings are posted on the Internet >>>

42

WHAT THE WORLD THINKS...

These are two articles from newspapers around the world commenting on Kenneth Bigley, held by terrorists in Iraq. Compare and contrast the viewpoints and see if you can find any more newspaper reports or other media discussing his kidnapping and death.

Arab News,
September 30, 2004

" A weeping British hostage was shown pleading for help between the bars of a makeshift cage in a video that surfaced yesterday, a sobering reminder of the grim reality for at least 18 foreign captives still held by Iraqi militants."

Mary Riddell,
The Observer,
September 26, 2004

"He called himself a man of little consequence. 'Mr. Blair, I am nothing to you,' he said. Kenneth Bigley was too modest. The lurid coverage of his ordeal has repelled and gripped a nation following every twist of a story infused with hope but always likely to end tragically. Abu Musab al-Zarqawi, the murderer of Mr. Bigley's two American housemates, plays a short and vile game."

Chapter 7

The Future of Terrorism

Terrorism is changing. Terrorist groups have become more sophisticated in terms of organizational structure, technological capability, methods of fund-raising, recruitment, and dissemination of propaganda. Another trend has been the alliance of terrorist groups with states.

One of the letters sent during the 2001 anthrax attacks in the U.S.A. The letters, laced with lethal spores, were mailed to two senators and several news media offices. It is feared that in the future, terrorist groups might increasingly use such methods.

State-Sponsored Terrorism

Today, states such as Iran and Syria are using terrorist groups as a means of waging war and pursuing foreign policy objectives covertly and anonymously. For example, Iran sponsors Shi'ite insurgents in Iraq who are attacking Sunni and U.S. forces there. It may be that future wars will be conducted by states using terrorists as surrogate warriors.

New Weapons

In the future, terrorists may turn to weapons of mass destruction (WMD). There have been sporadic examples of WMD usage, such as the 1990 chlorine gas attack by Tamil Tigers, but the manufacture and delivery of weapons remains difficult. Nevertheless, WMD remains attractive to terrorists because of its psychological impact. Even small-casualty attacks like the 2001 anthrax scare in the U.S.A., which killed five, can cause widespread fear and alarm.

Counterterrorism

As the struggle against international terrorism continues, states are becoming increasingly sophisticated in their ability to break up terrorist cells and preempt attacks. This has been made possible partly by improved security systems, as well as by better human intelligence—information gathered from surveillance, spies, moles, and prisoners. As a result,

Animal rights protestors on a march employ one of the more peaceful methods to achieve their aims.

the U.S. government claims that at least ten major terrorist attacks were thwarted between 2002 and 2006.

Future Causes

As one type of terrorism gradually diminishes, other forms are likely to take its place. Today, major issues include religion and national identity. Tomorrow, terrorists might be stirred by other causes. Already, some environmental, animal rights, and antiglobalization groups are using terrorist tactics.

Will terrorism always be with us? As long as groups exist that are sufficiently angered by a particular issue and feel powerless to bring about change except through violence, the answer is probably "yes." However, the lessons we are learning in the fight against terrorism today may well help us to confront it effectively in the future.

Abu Sayyaf An Islamist terrorist group operating in the southern Philippines.

Al-Aqsa Intifada A Palestinian uprising against the Israeli occupation of the West Bank and Gaza Strip that took place between 2000 and 2005.

al Qaeda An international alliance of Sunni Islamist terrorist organizations, founded by Osama bin Laden in Afghanistan in 1989.

al Qaeda in Iraq A terrorist group, originally known as Tawhid and Jihad, active in the Iraqi insurgency, formerly led by Abu Musab al-Zarquawi.

ANC The African National Congress is a movement that fought against apartheid in South Africa.

Angry Brigade A left-wing terrorist group responsible for a series of bomb attacks in the UK between 1970 and 1972.

anthrax Bacterial disease of mammals, especially cattle and sheep, transmittable to humans through inhalation, digestion, or cuts in the skin.

antiglobalization Opposition to globalization—the increasing global integration and interdependence of economic, social, and cultural life.

Army of God A Christian, right-wing terrorist group based in the southern U.S.A. that has launched a number of attacks on abortion clinics.

Aum Shinrikyo A Japanese religious group now known as Aleph, which conducted a number of terrorist attacks in the 1990s.

Black September A Palestinian nationalist terrorist group founded by members of Fatah in 1970.

caliphate The caliph was a title taken by Muslim rulers in the time of the Islamic and Ottoman empires. The caliphate was the territory over which the caliph's rule extended.

capitalist An economic system characterized by a free competitive market and based on private ownership of the means of production.

chlorine gas A heavy, greenish-yellow gas that can be used as a chemical weapon.

civil liberties The basic rights guaranteed to citizens by law, such as freedom of speech.

Cold War The state of nonviolent conflict between the Soviet Union and the United States and their respective allies between 1945 and 1990.

communist A system, or the belief in a system, in which capitalism is overthrown and control of wealth and property resides with the state.

counterrevolutionary Describing right-wing forces that fight against revolution.

cyberterrorism A form of terrorism in which computer systems are attacked or threatened.

Direct Action A Canadian left-wing terrorist group active in the early 1980s.

EOKA Ethniki Organosis Kyprion Agoniston was a Greek Cypriot nationalist terrorist group that fought for the removal of UK troops and for union with Greece in the mid-to-late 1950s.

ETA Euskadi Ta Askatasuna is a nationalist terrorist group based in Spain that fights for Basque independence.

ethnic minority A group with a similar cultural background that forms a minority in a country.

Fatah A major Palestinian political party and the largest organization in the PLO.

FLN The Front de Libération Nationale was an Algerian nationalist terrorist group that fought for Algerian independence from France in the 1950s and early 1960s.

fundamentalist A religious movement based on a strict interpretation of holy writings.

GIA The Group Islamique Armé is an Islamist terrorist group that wants to overthrow the Algerian government and replace with an Islamic state.

guerilla A member of an unofficial military force, usually with some political objective such as the overthrow of a government.

Hezbollah A Shi'ite Islamist political organization based in Lebanon that wishes to impose Islamic rule in Lebanon and eliminate Israel.

homophobic Hating or fearing homosexuals.

ideology A system of beliefs that forms the basis of a social, economic, or political philosophy or program.

infidels An Islamist term for people who do not believe in Islam.

insurgency An uprising against a government.

IRA An Irish nationalist organization that used terrorism between 1969 and 1997 in its struggle to end British rule in Northern Ireland.

Irgun A Jewish nationalist terrorist group, operating between 1931 and 1948, that fought to end British rule in Palestine and the establishment of the state of Israel.

Islamism A strict form of Islam based on a literal interpretation of the Koran and other holy Islamic scriptures.

Jewish Defense League A U.S.-based Jewish terrorist organization created in 1968 by Rabbi Meir Kahane.

jihad The struggle for Islam. This can be interpreted either as a holy war, or as a spiritual striving.

left-wing Supporting the idea of political or social changes or reform.

martyrdom attack An Islamist term for a suicide attack, in which a person strapped with explosives deliberately blows themselves up in a crowded place.

mujahideen An Arabic term for Muslims fighting a war or involved in any other struggle.

national self-determination The ability or right of a people to exist as a nation without interference from an occupying power.

nationalist Belief in the right of one's people to exist as a nation, or (in the case of right-wing nationalism) belief in the status of one's nation above all others.

New Left A term used to describe left-wing movements of the 1960s and 1970s that emphasized the need for political activism, such as demonstrations, boycotts, street marches, strikes, and civil disobedience.

PFLP-EO The Popular Front for the Liberation of Palestine-External Operations was a breakaway group from the Palestinian nationalist terrorist organization, the PFLP.

PKK The Partiya Karkeren Kurdistan, or Kurdistan Workers Party, is a Kurdish nationalist terrorist group founded in the 1970s.

PLO The Palestine Liberation Organization is a confederation of organizations, founded in 1964, whose goal is the establishment of a Palestinian state.

Red Army Faction The Red Army Faction, also known as the Baader-Meinhof Gang, was a German left-wing terrorist group that operated from 1970 to 1998.

Red Brigades The Red Brigades (Brigate Rosse) was an Italian left-wing terrorist group active during the 1970s and 1980s.

revolutionary vanguard A group who are foremost in a movement to overthrow a government or political system.

right-wing Supporting the idea of maintaining social and political systems as they are.

RZ Revolutionare Zellen (Revolutionary Cells) was a group of German left-wing terrorist cells.

sharia law Islamic religious law, based on the Koran.

Shia The branch of Islam that considers Ali, a relative of Muhammad, and his descendents to be Muhammad's true successors.

socialist Relating to, or belief in, a political system in which wealth is shared equally between people, and the main industries and trade are controlled by the government.

Soviet Union A country consisting of Russia and a number of other East European, Baltic, and Central Asian countries, which existed from 1922 to 1991.

steganography The art of writing hidden messages in such a way that no one apart from the intended recipient knows of the existence of the message.

Sunni The largest branch of Islam, which believes in the traditions of Sunna and accepts the first four caliphs as rightful successors to Muhammad.

superpower A nation with greater political, economic, or military power than most or all other nations.

surrogate Taking the place of someone or something else.

Tamil Tigers The Liberation Tigers of Tamil Eelam (LTTE) is a Tamil nationalist terrorist organization that wishes to create a separate Tamil state in the north and east of Sri Lanka.

Tawhid and Jihad A terrorist group active in the insurgency in Iraq. It gradually became known as al Qaeda in Iraq.

totalitarian Relating to a centralized government system in which a single party controls all political, economic, social, and cultural life.

tsar An emperor of Russia before 1917.

UN The United Nations is an organization of nations, formed in 1945, to promote peace, security, and international cooperation.

Vietnam War A war fought by the U.S.A. in Vietnam between 1964 and 1975.

weapons of mass destruction Chemical, biological, and nuclear weapons.

Weathermen A U.S. left-wing terrorist organization whose aim was to achieve the revolutionary overthrow of the government of the U.S.A.

Zapatistas The Zapatista Army of National Liberation is a left-wing terrorist group based in Chiapas, one of the poorest states of Mexico.

BOOKS

Combating Terrorism
by Jane Marie Bedell
(Compass Point Books, 2010)

Facts on File Library of World History: Encyclopedia of Terrorism
by Cindy C. Combs and Martin W. Slann
(Facts on File, 2007)

Why Are People Terrorists?
by Alex Woolf
(Heinemann-Raintree, 2005)

WEB SITES

Due to the changing nature of Internet links, Rosen Publishing has developed an online list of Web sites related to the subject of this book. This site is regularly updated. Please use this link to access this list: http://www.rosenlinks.com/glo/terr